Life
on Purpose

A Practical Tool for Crafting a God-honoring,
Joy-producing Personal Mission Statement

Michael Acker

Printed in the United States of America

Print ISBN: 978-1-954024-53-3
eBook ISBN: 978-1-954024-54-0

https://www.goonthemission.com

To contact, please e-mail:
Michael.Acker@goonthemission.com

Table of Contents

Brothers and sisters, I do not consider myself yet to have taken hold of [my goal]. But one thing I do: Forgetting what is behind and straining toward what is ahead, I press on toward the goal to win the prize for which God has called me heavenward in Christ Jesus.

PHILIPPIANS 3:13–14 (NIV)

"Would you tell me, please, which way I ought to go from here?" [asked Alice.]

"That depends a good deal on where you want to get to," said the Cat.

"I don't much care where–" said Alice.

"Then it doesn't matter which way you go," said the Cat.

LEWIS CARROLL, THROUGH THE LOOKING-GLASS

Introduction

At this moment, who do you relate to more, the Apostle Paul with a laser focus on his destination or Alice wandering aimlessly around?

The latter is fine for characters in a children's book but, as followers of Christ, we are called to so much more—something deeper, more meaningful, and inherently tied to eternity. Something that is ultimately much more rewarding and joy-filled than binging Netflix or retiring at fifty and playing golf every day.

My life has been a series of twists and turns, from son of drug smugglers to pastor to corporate trainer to executive director, but every step has been purposeful and has led me to where I am. Much of that is God's grace—He has never let me out His hands. But my choices also played a role. As Paul wrote:

> Therefore, my dear friends, as you have always obeyed—not only in my presence, but now much more in my absence—continue to work out your salvation with fear and trembling, for it is God who works in you to will and to act in order to fulfill His good purpose (Philippians 2:12–13 NIV).

As a young adult, I intentionally watched men and women who were successful personally, professionally, and spiritually so I could emulate them. Something I saw again and again was purposefulness—their success was never the result of luck, but intentional choices. Like Paul, they had a laser focus on their mission.

Following their example, I wrote my first mission statement at age eighteen and have updated it every four to five years. And as a pastor and a coach to C-suite executives, I've always pushed my congregation, staff, and clients to do the same.

This book distills my years of study and experience into an interactive guide to help you navigate your inner landscape to discover God's purpose for you and develop your own mission statement.

You can download printable worksheets from this book at our "mission vault."

https://vault.goonthemission.com

Don't let its small size fool you, this material has made a major impact on me and the people I've worked with. The journey will require honesty, careful reflection, and a willingness to dig deep. As I said, it's an interactive guide. You'll need to listen to the "still, small voice" and hear what God has to say about your identity and purpose—in a world that often communicates the opposite.

Before you're finished, you'll have your own, thoughtfully created Personal Mission Statement to guide how you live each day and where you'll be ten years from now.
Let this be your workbook for the soul, a personal retreat that you can return to time and again. As you progress, you may find yourself revisiting it, redefining goals, and refining the expression of your mission as you evolve.

Alongside this booklet, I've created free resources designed to complement and enhance your experience such as identifying and using your spiritual gifts.

https://vault.goonthemission.com

May you find in these pages the courage to embrace your God-given calling and the inspiration to live out the mission He designed just for you!

— Michael Acker

So God created mankind in His own image, in the image of God He created them; male and female He created them.

GENESIS 1:27 (NIV)

Today you are You, that is truer than true. There is no one alive who is Youer than You.

DR. SUESS

Tailor-Made Mission

If you're a teacher or the parent of more than one child, you know how different each one is and how they require a unique approach. Even identical twins can have entirely different personalities and learning styles.

The same is true of you and your God-given mission. We were made in God's image, but, just as a prism splits light up into different colors, we all reflect a different aspect of His image—and it takes all of us working together to get a better picture of what God is like in all His splendor. Or to use another analogy, we all have to work together to be a fully functioning Body (see 1 Corinthians 12:12–27)

It's easy to lose sight of your God-given identity and calling amid the world's clamor and chaos. To live a life crafted by divine design, you must first seek God's priorities for you and uncover the elements that form the essence of your God-reflected "you-ness."

Crafting a Personal Mission Statement is a powerful way to engage in deep communion with yourself and with God, to clarify your priorities and solidify your identity in Him and your role in His mission—as distinct from someone else's. Like David trying to wear King Saul's armor, you'll never be at your best trying to be someone else or carry out their specific mission.

Remember, your relationship with Christ is both discovered and nurtured; it's dynamic, growing as you walk in obedience and faith. A Personal Mission Statement is, therefore, a declaration of the values and purposes that God has impressed upon your heart.

In crafting a comprehensive mission statement, I will guide you with thoughtful questions that promote spiritual reflection, times of prayer, and offer biblical insights that will light your path. Journey with me, and by the time we reach the end, you will hold a Personal Mission Statement that resonates with the heart of God for your life.

The steps we'll take together are rooted in Scripture and spiritual discipline:

- Committing your path to the Lord
- Gaining clarity on the vision God has for you
- Discerning your true, God-honoring values
- Understanding the good works God has prepared for you to do
- Organizing your thoughts through prayerful reflection
- Drafting your Personal Mission Statement
- Reviewing and refining it through the lens of Scripture

Finally, there's no single prescribed way to walk this path. You may choose to embark on this journey swiftly, in the space of a day, watch alongside some of our free video content, do as a small group, or you may work through it over many months. What matters most is that you seek a space for prayerful contemplation, where you can listen for God's voice and allow His Spirit to guide you without interruption.

Embrace this journey with an open heart, and may you find joy in every step you take with the Lord!

Have I not commanded you? Be strong and courageous. Do not be afraid; do not be discouraged, for the LORD your God will be with you wherever you go.

JOSHUA 1:9 (NIV)

Everything is safe which we commit to Him, and nothing is really safe which is not so committed.

A.W. TOZER

Committed

Our minds often hesitate until we make a
full commitment, whether it's embracing
a new role at work, making a big move, or
establishing a Personal Mission Statement.
Until you're fully committed, the ease of
retreat can prevent you from putting your
whole heart into the effort, and any small
hurdle may topple your best-laid plans.

But when you say with conviction, "I am doing
this and will not be stopped," a shift occurs.
You begin to see God's hand at work, guiding
you toward your goal. Distractions fade away,
focus narrows from the 'what-ifs' to the 'how-
tos,' and the path forward becomes clearer.
Opportunities arise, unforeseen help arrives,
and a renewed energy surges within you.

As we set out on this work of discovery, it's vital
that you promise to see this journey through.
Commit to completing this guide and creating
your Personal Mission Statement.

Personal Mission Statement

I commit to invest the time and energy needed to develop a Personal Mission Statement that will help me uncover, shape, and understand my purpose.

This matters to me, and I am fully committed because...

_____

_____

_____

_____

Signed: _____

Date: _____

Jesus replied, "No one who puts a hand to the plow and looks back is fit for service in the kingdom of God."

LUKE 9:62 (NIV)

If you want to experience the release of the power of God, you have to make a decisive dedication to your purpose. That's your 'burn the ships' moment.

TONY EVANS

Passion-Driven Vision

We each harbor dreams of what the future might hold. Close your eyes, and you might easily envision where you hope to be in five years. But be honest: are they daydreams—a collection of 'someday...'—or true vision?

Vision can be described as a clear picture of a desired future, serving as a strategic roadmap to achieve specific outcomes, and true vision is typically grounded in realistic aspirations.

Vision is where you want to go. Mission is how you get there. Do you have a passionate vision that informs and motivates your actions today?

As Proverbs (29:18) says, "Without vision, the people perish." A God-directed vision is a driving force, stirring up a passion to fulfill your ongoing mission. This passion is more than a fleeting desire; it's an integral part of who you are and what you ultimately stand for. It's the unique mark you're supposed to make on the world and the legacy you'll leave.

Clearly, fulfilling your purpose doesn't earn you God's approval or love. Even if my son never moves out of the house and spends his days playing video games, I'll love him the same. But

I want so much more for him than that. In the same way, God gives you a mission designed just for you that provides an overarching purpose to your life.

I speak of 'PASSION-DRIVEN VISION' because that type of vision acts as a potent, inner voice that guides us. So foundational to your being, this passion shapes every decision, urging you forward towards your goals, and provides the discernment to know when to embrace opportunities or when to walk away, all in alignment with your core priorities.

Such passion emboldens you to confront even your greatest fears. It can dispel doubts. It can quieten the voices of discouragement.

1. Identify any fears or doubts that may hinder your progress towards a clearer vision for your life. How can you address them?

_____

_____

_____

_____

_____

_____

2 If you were to ask family and friends to identify areas of passion in your life, what would they say? Would you agree with their assessment?

_____

_____

_____

_____

_____

_____

3 Reflect on a time when your passion led you to act. What was the outcome, and what did you learn about yourself?

_____

_____

_____

_____

_____

_____

_____

_____

_____

4 If you feel like your passion has dwindled, then think back to a time when your passion was high. What were you doing? What were you involved in? What actions ignite God-given passion in your life?

_____

_____

_____

_____

_____

_____

_____

_____

_____

Don't worry if your current level of passion is not where you think it should be. That is how this guide will help you. If you feel stuck at any point, pause, pray, and move on to the next prompt.

Therefore, since we are surrounded by such a great cloud of witnesses, let us throw off everything that hinders and the sin that so easily entangles. And let us run with perseverance the race marked out for us, fixing our eyes on Jesus, the pioneer and perfecter of faith.

HEBREWS 12:1-3 (NIV)

Leadership is not about titles, positions, or flowcharts. It is about one life influencing another.

JOHN C. MAXWELL

Shapers of Mission

Rick Warren, the author of The Purpose Driven Life, profoundly influenced my understanding of life's purpose when I was twenty-two years old. His teachings went beyond simply knowing personality traits to discovering one's role in the grand tapestry of God's design. He presented the concept that each of us is shaped by God's overarching purpose for our life, and this understanding guides not only what we do but also who we become.

Though my specific mission differs from Warren's, his dedication to guiding others in finding their purpose inspired my own mission. I may not share his exact approach, but his commitment to empowering others has shaped the way I seek to impact the world — by helping others find their place and encouraging them to embrace their mission with courage.

Influence is inevitable; it sculpts our perspectives and can guide our steps. The key lies in selecting influences that align with the mission we believe we are called to fulfill. It's not about imitation but about finding inspiration in their footsteps that resonate with our unique journey.

1 First, thinking in broad strokes, in what areas do you find yourself most influenced? Education, work choices, finances, entertainment, faith, somewhere else?

_____

_____

_____

_____

_____

_____

_____

2 Reflecting on your life, what significant events have profoundly impacted and molded you?

_____

_____

_____

_____

_____

_____

Life on Purpose

Follow my example, as I follow the
example of Christ.

1 CORINTHIANS 11:1 (NIV)

Leaders become great not because of
their power, but because of their ability
to empower others.

JOHN C. MAXWELL

Examine the Exemplary

1 Create a list of some of the most influential people in your life.

_____

_____

_____

_____

_____

_____

Circle the one who had the most profound positive influence on you.

2 What do you admire and appreciate most about them? Why?

_____

_____

_____

_____

_____

_____

3 What do you consider as their greatest success?

_____

_____

_____

_____

_____

_____

_____

_____

4 If you could adopt one thing from them personally and another from their achievements, what would it be?

_____

_____

_____

_____

_____

_____

For we are God's handiwork, created in Christ Jesus to do good works, which God prepared in advance for us to do.

EPHESIANS 2:10 (NIV)

God doesn't require us to succeed; he only requires that you try.

MOTHER TERESA

Realizing Your Potential

Remember, in God's grand design, among the billions, He created only one of you. Envision the best version of yourself through God's eyes. Set aside your shortcomings. Who are you at your finest, authentically you, not a copy of another?

One of the pivotal moments in my own leadership journey comes from a conversation I had with a man named John. Coming to me as his pastor, he shared his regret, feeling as though he had missed his calling to make an impactful difference.

"I was always told I had potential," he confided, "and it feels like it's gone unfulfilled."

John had served faithfully in the Navy, achieving the esteemed rank of Chief Petty Officer, yet he wondered if he should have pursued being a motivational speaker, a pastor, or an author. Inquiring further about his service, it became clear that his leadership positively influenced countless individuals— more than many in conventional pastoral or similar roles.

"Do you relish the thought of influencing others?" I probed.

"That's just it, I feel I've let that slip by!" he lamented.

I asked him to reflect on the number of lives he's touched weekly. It dawned on both of us that his service had already crafted a profound legacy.

John's naval career began not from a place of spiritual fervor but from a search for direction and a call to duty. Yet, as we explored the breadth of his impact, he began to see the impact he had already been making and the continued potential for his future.

John might have excelled in other vocations, but dwelling on what might have been was not fruitful. What mattered was the realization that he was already able to live on purpose by identifying his mission and seeing how he could live that out in his current capacity. He realized he didn't need to go back or do something different. He was capable of creating lasting change in the lives he touched daily.

1 Is there an area where you identify with John's experience? Where do you feel you fell short of your potential?

_____

_____

_____

_____

_____

_____

2 Take this further and consider other places in life where you feel 'benched'? Like a talented athlete sitting on the sidelines, do you feel like some of your abilities are out of use?

_____

_____

_____

_____

_____

_____

_____

Each one should use whatever gift he has received to serve others, faithfully administering God's grace in its various forms.

1 PETER 4:10 (NIV)

The place God calls you to is the place where your deep gladness and the world's deep hunger meet.

FREDERICK BUECHNER

Realizing Your Potential
(continued)

Every instance where someone expresses to me their fear of missed potential, I'm reminded of my dialogue with John. Rather than aspiring to emulate another, strive to excel as yourself and acknowledge the influence you wield in your current station.

1 Consider ten characteristics that most authentically represent who you are:

1. _____

2. _____

3. _____

4. _____

5. _____

6. _____

7. _____

8. _____

9. _____

10. _____

2 Reflect on moments when you felt most confident and accomplished. What personal qualities or attributes do you think contributed to those successes?

_____

_____

_____

_____

_____

_____

3 Consider times when you've faced adversity or obstacles. How have your personal strengths and qualities helped you overcome these challenges?

_____

_____

_____

_____

_____

_____

_____

Therefore, if anyone is in Christ, the new creation has come: The old has gone, the new is here!

2 CORINTHIANS 5:17-19 (NIV)

The best thing about the future is that it comes one day at a time.

ABRAHAM LINCOLN

Life on Purpose

Choose Your Destination

Take time to choose who you are becoming.
...the talents you wish to cultivate.
...the character you want to embody.
...the lifestyle you aim to lead.
...the person you want to be when no one is looking.

By considering those who exemplify the virtues you admire and your own aspirations you set a compass for your journey.

For instance:
· I am respected the most by the people closest to me.
· I am dedicated to being fully present for my friends and family.
· I turn to prayer instead of worry.
· I work hard as for the Lord rather than for people (Col 3:23-24).

Envision the traits you desire to develop and fulfill through this life. Phrase your objectives not as distant dreams but as steps you are actively taking. For example, express "I work hard," rather than "I will work hard." The more you believe the truth of where God is leading you, the more you will consciously and subconsciously move towards it.

_____

_____

_____

_____

_____

_____

_____

_____

_____

_____

_____

_____

_____

Do not conform to the pattern of this world, but be transformed by the renewing of your mind. Then you will be able to test and approve what God's will is—his good, pleasing and perfect will.

ROMANS 12:2 (NIV)

True faith means holding nothing back. It means putting every hope in God's fidelity to His Promises.

FRANCIS CHAN

Becoming

Continue mapping out your future character destination by answering the following questions. Make sure to write your statements as though this is already who you are.

1 My personal strengths are...

_____

_____

_____

_____

_____

2 My strongest abilities include...

_____

_____

_____

_____

_____

_____

3 My best character traits are...

_____
_____
_____
_____
_____
_____
_____

4 Those who know me well would say that I excel in...

_____
_____
_____
_____
_____
_____
_____
_____

Life on Purpose

And Jesus grew in wisdom and stature, and in favor with God and man.

LUKE 2:52 (NIV)

What we are is God's gift to us. What we become is our gift to God.

ELEANOR POWELL

Foundational Values

Identify your core values, the fundamental beliefs and principles that guide your life. Consider these values not just as words, but as the pillars of your daily existence, the non-negotiable elements that direct your decisions and actions.

Your core values don't have to be your currently lived values, they can be aspirational if you understand why you resonate with it.

Take a moment to pray and identify the values you hold to and gravitate towards.

Look at this list to find inspiration and think beyond these to choose ones that reflect who you are.

1. **Physical health** - Treating your body as a temple and cherishing wellness.
2. **Kindness** - Extending a hand of friendship and warmth in every interaction.
3. **Advocacy** - Standing up for what you believe in and championing causes.
4. **Freedom** - Valuing independence and the power to choose your own path.
5. **Enjoyable hobbies** - Embracing pastimes that bring joy and fulfillment.
6. **Faith** - Holding fast to spiritual convictions that anchor your soul.

7. **Authenticity -** Being true to yourself in all aspects of life.
8. **Peace of mind -** Seeking tranquility and balance amidst life's storms.
9. **Family -** Prioritizing the bonds and love shared with family members.
10. **Friendships -** Cultivating relationships that enrich and support you.
11. **Education -** Pursuing knowledge and wisdom as lifelong endeavors.
12. **Personal fulfillment -** Achieving a sense of accomplishment in your pursuits.
13. **Honor -** Living a life marked by integrity and respectability.
14. **Money -** Recognizing financial stability as a tool for facilitating other values.
15. **Happiness -** Pursuing what brings you inner joy and contentment.
16. **Security -** Seeking safety and stability in your personal and professional life.
17. **Laughter -** Finding humor and light-heartedness as a source of strength and resilience.
18. **Compassion -** Embracing empathy and caring for others' well-being.
19. **Service -** Committing to the betterment of others and contributing to the community.
20. **Resilience -** Cultivating the ability to recover from adversities with strength.
21. **Integrity -** Ensuring your actions are consistent with your moral and ethical beliefs.

22. **Creativity -** Valuing innovative thinking and expressing oneself through various forms.
23. **Wisdom -** Seeking deep understanding and the application of knowledge in life.
24. **Courage -** Demonstrating bravery to face challenges and stand up for your beliefs.
25. **Stewardship -** Taking responsibility for managing and caring for the resources entrusted to you.

Create your own list of values that don't show up on the list.

Narrow the list down to ten values and rate how important you want them to be to you.

Value   **Importance**

Now, take off ones that you think 'should be' and narrow it down to five values that resonate deeply with you, those that you feel are integral to who you are and how you want to live.

A good person leaves an inheritance for their children's children, but a sinner's wealth is stored up for the righteous.

PROVERBS 13:22 (NIV)

Generosity is the key to unlocking God's blessings. When we give freely and cheerfully, we experience the joy of sharing in God's abundance.

CHARLES STANLEY

Money Matters

Money is a powerful force in our lives. It can provide comfort and security, but it can also bring stress and anxiety. How we approach money also says a lot about how we will live our lives.

The Bible consistently refers to God's people as stewards. Which means that we don't own what we have (talents, abilities, opportunities, finances, etc.). Instead, we are managers entrusted to act as agents of God. Everything we create or earn comes from the abilities God has given us. We can easily begin to think that we are the only ones responsible for the good in our life. Moses corrected that in Deuteronomy 8:18 "But remember the LORD your God, for it is he who gives you the ability to produce wealth..."

Will we approach money as stewards or owners? Will we take credit and feel like we are in solely in charge or will we give thanks and be generous?

Not only does money reveal our approach to life, but how we manage money can reveal a lot about our values and priorities.

Jesus clearly states that where our treasure is our heart will follow (Matthew 6:21). So where is your treasure? If you were to categorize your spending, what would that say about you? What do you want it to say about you?

Take a moment to reflect on the role money plays in the way you live out your life and mission.

1 What are your core beliefs about money? Below I will guide you on some reflections, take this spot here to write freely about how you feel about money and the role it plays in your life.

_____

_____

_____

_____

_____

_____

_____

_____

_____

_____

2 Consider the messages you received about money while growing up and how they have influenced your financial attitudes and behaviors.

_____

_____

_____

_____

_____

_____

How does money align with your values?

3 Reflect on whether your financial choices and spending habits align with your deepest values and long-term goals.

_____

_____

_____

_____

_____

_____

What emotions does money evoke in you?

4 Explore your emotional relationship with money. Do you feel secure, anxious, or content when it comes to your financial situation?

_____

_____

_____

_____

_____

How can you use money as a tool for positive impact?

5 Think about ways you can use your financial resources to make a positive difference in your life and the lives of others.

_____

_____

_____

_____

_____

I have no greater joy than to hear that my children are walking in the truth.

3 JOHN 1:4 (NIV)

The only thing you take with you when you're gone is what you leave behind.

JOHN ALLSTON

Legacy Crafting

As you reflect on what you are writing and have written, imagine the enduring legacy these insights help you leave.

A legacy isn't merely what you leave for people; it's what you leave in them — the memories, the teachings, the acts, the feelings, and the impact that outlives your time on earth. Take time to record the legacy you aim to leave, one that's shaped by the personal truths you've uncovered.

Use these bullet points to help you craft the legacy you want to leave:

- What specific memories or teachings do you hope people will carry with them as part of your enduring legacy?
- How do you envision your actions and impact continuing to resonate with others long after you're gone?
- Consider the feelings or emotions you aim to inspire in those who come across you in this life.

_____

_____

_____

_____

_____

_____

_____

_____

_____

_____

_____

_____

_____

_____

_____

_____

_____

_____

_____

_____

Then Joseph said to them, 'Do not interpretations belong to God? Tell me your dreams.'

GENESIS 40:8 (NIV)

"

The size of your dreams must always exceed your current capacity to achieve them. If your dreams do not scare you, they are not big enough.

ELLEN JOHNSON SIRLEAF

Dreams Unleashed

Our minds often gravitate towards the tangible and the immediate needs of daily routines. That's needed much of the time, but passion that inspires a mission driven life needs more than mere practicality. To become passionate about your God-given mission it's imperative to tap into the space where dreams can run free.

When we unleash our imagination, we allow ourselves to wander, to dream with the boundlessness of Joseph in Genesis 37, whose visions foretold his future. Unleash your imagination and ask yourself not just what is, but what could be. Invite the "What if...?" to flourish before you ever consider the "How?"

1. Imagine a life where the job you worked wasn't for money but out of passion to contribute to the world. I would choose to work in/for...

_____

_____

_____

_____

_____

2 I choose this work because...

_____

_____

_____

_____

_____

3 The area (hobby, accomplishment, sport, etc) that excites me the most in life is...

_____

_____

_____

_____

4 It makes me feel...

_____

_____

_____

_____

_____

5 Now, imagine you suddenly had the supernatural to completely fix only one tangible problem in the world! I would fix...

_____

_____

_____

_____

6 When I let my mind wander beyond my duties and obligations, I imagine myself...

_____

_____

_____

_____

_____

_____

_____

_____

Commit to the Lord whatever you do, and he will establish your plans.

PROVERBS 16:3 (NIV)

Aim at heaven and you will get earth thrown in. Aim at earth and you get neither.

C.S. LEWIS

Inspirational Goals

After passionate dreaming, understanding your strengths, identifying your values and reflecting on what makes you you, the stage is set to chart your God-given ambitions by clarifying your goals.

What milestones do you aspire to reach? What do you want to accomplish? What will you "do"? What kind of adventures will you go on? What will you leave behind? Who will you impact?

Clarifying your life's aims will sharpen your focus and direct your energies like the blinders on a racehorse, ensuring you charge towards the finish line without distraction. Establishing clear objectives turns your aspirations into targets to aim for with dedication and vigor.

When I was eighteen, I was inspired by John Goddard's 'Life List' – an ambitious set of 127 goals he chose at just fifteen. Far from the mundane, his list was filled with the audacious spirit of adventure: scaling peaks, voyaging down the Amazon, delving into the works of great philosophers, venturing into medical service, and even dreaming of lunar exploration. Of his list, he accomplished 110 feats.

You don't need to adopt Goddard's 127 goals or his specific dreams. But let his example ignite your own creativity. Be inspired to pave a unique path – be the pioneer of your journey, the original you.

In the next section, you'll compile a more extensive list. To get you started, dream up one lofty goal. Think of one large bucket list item and write about what it mean to accomplish it.

_____

_____

_____

_____

_____

_____

_____

_____

_____

_____

Then the Lord replied: 'Write down the revelation and make it plain on tablets so that a herald may run with it...'

HABAKKUK 2:2-3 (NIV)

Set goals that don't feel all that comfortable and give God something to work with.

BOB GOFF

Write Out Your Goals

Transition now from the broad strokes of dreaming to the fine lines of action. Find a place where distractions fade and your thoughts can be organized. Here, you'll draft a catalog of goals that resonate with your soul. Pray that God guides your planning.

Be precise in your planning. Your goals don't need to match John Goddard's adventures or anyone else' actions. Let your goals be authentic to you and your relationship with Christ. Your goals are the action-oriented future mirror of your values and visions:

Here are some examples to help you go from lofty dream to actionable goals:
- Craft and publish a memoir that tells future generations about how God changed my life.
- Take a mission trip to Senegal, West Africa to build a school.
- Spend a weekend in the mountains with three close friends.
- Give $50,000 to causes close to your heart over the next five years.
- Celebrate your grandkids getting baptized.
- Lead a specific friend or family member to know Jesus.

_____

_____

_____

_____

_____

_____

_____

_____

_____

_____

_____

_____

_____

_____

_____

_____

_____

_____

_____

_____

_____

_____

_____

_____

_____

_____

_____

_____

_____

_____

_____

This is the day the Lord has made; let us rejoice and be glad in it.

PSALM 118:24 (NIV)

You have been given a great gift, your life. What will you do with it?

BILLY GRAHAM

Define Your Perfect Day

Take a moment to center your thoughts and project yourself into the future. Envision your perfect day—the kind of day that you would label as your best. Consider when this day takes place, the setting, the series of events, and the people who accompany you. Dive into the details of what makes this particular day stand out. Is it the activities, the conversations, the feelings of accomplishment, or the simple joys that define its perfection? Explore the reasons this day resonates as your dream day.

Begin to jot down your thoughts:
- The date or season of my ideal day:
- The location where I am:
- The main events that unfold:
- The individuals who are with me:
- The reasons this day feels ideal:

The more detailed your description, the clearer your vision becomes. Use this exercise to align your daily actions with the path to your ideal day.

_____

_____

_____

_____

_____

_____

_____

_____

_____

_____

_____

_____

_____

_____

_____

_____

_____

_____

_____

_____

_____

_____

_____

_____

_____

_____

_____

_____

_____

_____

_____

_____

_____

_____

Trust in the Lord with all your heart and lean not on your own understanding; in all your ways submit to Him, and He will make your paths straight.

PROVERBS 3:5-6 (NIV)

The purpose of life is not to be happy. It is to be useful, to be honorable, to be compassionate, to have it make some difference that you have lived and lived well.

RALPH WALDO EMERSON

Compass Points

Drawing from years of pastoral experience and time spent in speaking and coaching, I've come to recognize certain elements that give a Personal Mission Statement its life-changing power.

A truly inspiring statement will:
1. Define your life's purpose and what you are driven to achieve.
2. Reflect your deepest convictions and core values.
3. Paint a vivid picture of the future you're working towards.
4. List specific, attainable goals that align with your vision.
5. Incorporate your passions, highlighting what excites and motivates you.
6. Identify your unique strengths and how you can leverage them.
7. Acknowledge areas for growth and how you plan to develop them.
8. Detail the impact you want to have on others and your community.
9. Describe the legacy you hope to leave and how you will be remembered.
10. Commit to actionable steps that bring your mission to life every day.

Your Personal Mission Statement is not just a declaration of intent; it's a roadmap for your life's journey, a compass that guides you to your true north. Before you go to the next page, revisit, and add to any area you are missing. Examine what you have written through the lens of these ten compass points.

As you revisit what you have written, do you see any trends or themes? Write them down here:

_____

_____

_____

_____

_____

_____

_____

_____

_____

_____

_____

_____

_____

_____

_____

_____

_____

_____

_____

_____

_____

_____

_____

_____

_____

_____

_____

These commandments that I give you today are to be on your hearts. Impress them on your children. Talk about them when you sit at home and when you walk along the road, when you lie down and when you get up. Tie them as symbols on your hands and bind them on your foreheads. Write them on the doorframes of your houses and on your gates.

DEUTERONOMY 6:6-9 (NIV)

The purpose of your life is far greater than your own personal fulfillment, your peace of mind, or even your happiness. It's far greater than your family, your career, or even your wildest dreams and ambitions. If you want to know why you were placed on this planet, you must begin with God. You were born by His purpose and for His purpose.

RICK WARREN

Inspirational Examples

On the next couple of pages, I included many sample Personal Mission Statements. Some of these are imagined examples, others are hypothetical examples based on what I know about someone (such as C.S. Lewis).

I include these for your inspiration, not as template. There is no right or wrong answer. Read through these and see how these could potentially guide your own life.

When I first did this exercise at eighteen, I only wrote down three word: coach, pastor, mentor.

Later I rewrote my mission statement, and it increased in length and became "To reach people with the Love of God. Teach them who He is. Train people to reach and teach. Release them to train others outside of my sphere of influence. Repeat this process to amplify God's love and teachings."

This version is more thorough...but not easy to remember, so I've simplified it: Reach, Teach, Train Up, Release, and Repeat.

I've also reimagined it and expanded it. While

the words have changed through the years, the mission has remained. My own mission statement has played key roles in my choices, jobs, volunteer positions and more. A great personal mission statement will guide you and reorient you to your role in God's great mission.

Take inspiration from these and then it will be time to work on your personal mission statement.

To inspire people to live a purpose-driven life based on the teachings of Christ.

- Rick Warren (author of
"The Purpose Driven Life")

—————————————

I will use my skills in healthcare to heal and comfort the sick as Jesus did, showing compassion and care at every opportunity.

—————————————

- Embody Christ's teachings to foster peace and reconciliation.
- Actively engage in community dialogues to understand diverse perspectives.
- Facilitate unity by creating forums for open, respectful conversation.

- Volunteer for local initiatives that promote healing and togetherness.
- Mentor individuals in conflict resolution grounded in biblical principles.
- Support charitable causes that work towards community restoration.
- Lead by example in demonstrating forgiveness and collaboration.
- Pray regularly for the healing of divisions within the community and beyond.

———————————

To create music that brings people closer to God and encourages them in their faith journey.

> – Chris Tomlin (Christian musician)

———————————

I dedicate my life to embodying the teachings of Christ in every facet of my existence. I will strive to be an instrument of God's peace, to bring healing where there is hurt, to offer forgiveness where there is offense, and to radiate joy where there is sadness. My vocation is to be a living testament to His grace, encouraging others to discover their purpose and live it out in their communities.

To be an entrepreneur whose business practices are rooted in integrity, generosity, and stewardship, glorifying God through ethical success.

————————————

Proclaim the Gospel of Jesus Christ with clarity and passion, to lead by example in both word and deed, and to bring hope to the lost by demonstrating God's unfailing love for all humanity.
> – Billy Graham (based on his speaking and writing)

————————————

I dedicate my life to protecting God's creation, advocating for the environment, and teaching others to steward the Earth responsibly.

————————————

Serve the poorest of the poor with the love and compassion of Christ, to see the face of Jesus in every person I meet, and to be His hands and feet in a world that is in desperate need of care and comfort.
> – Mother Teresa (reflective of her life's work)

To pursue justice and equality for all God's children, using nonviolent methods to inspire change and foster a society where every person can live in harmony and have equal opportunity.

> - Martin Luther King Jr. (paraphrased from his teachings and public life)

———————————

Explore and explain the deeper truths of faith through writing and teaching, to defend the tenets of Christianity with reason and imagination, and to encourage others to see the joy and beauty in a life lived in relationship with God.

> - C.S. Lewis (hypothetical example based on his writings)

———————————

To protect and care for the abandoned and the needy, especially children, showing them the love of Christ, and to challenge others to give their lives in service to the kingdom of God.

> – Amy Carmichael (my take based on her work)

- I reach out to ensure people feel included.
- I teach people to help them know their value.
- I train people to realize their potential.
- I release people to go beyond me and stand on my shoulders.
- I repeat this process with the people around me.
- I lead my family to laugh a lot, thank God for everything, and follow Jesus.
- And when I fall or fail, by God's grace, I get up again.

> - Mike Acker (expanded mission statement)

These are samples to provide inspiration. As observed, Personal Mission Statements often come across in short paragraph form. When it comes to writing down your statement do what is best for you. Write it as a poem, or bullet points, or story, or song. Anything that speaks to you and for you.

God saw all that He had made,
and it was very good.

GENESIS 1:31A (NIV)

God is the ultimate Creator, and we, being
made in His image, have the
privilege of reflecting His creativity
in our own unique ways.

UNKNOWN

Reflect and Act

Go back and review your answers. Add or edit as needed. Now, put yourself in a creative brainstorm mode.

Put on music, go for a walk, sit down at a café, or stand at a whiteboard. Be ready to create in your best environment. You are going to engage in free writing where you write out everything and anything that pops into your mind regarding your purpose, God's plan for your life, your passion, life-long prayers and your God-given mission in this life. No editing. Don't worry about grammar or even full sentences. Don't censor yourself, just get all those thoughts out.

Put on a timer for five minutes. Breathe. Pray. GO!

_____

_____

_____

_____

_____

_____

_____

_____

_____

_____

_____

_____

_____

_____

_____

_____

_____

_____

_____

_____

_____

_____

_____

But be doers of the word, and not hearers only, deceiving yourselves.

JAMES 1:22 (NIV)

Prayer is the foundation for all action; it's where we get our orders from headquarters.

CORRIE TEN BOOM

Bring it All Together

The previous free-writing experience can bring out lots of ideas, subconscious dreams, God inspired direction, and non-related thoughts. It's time to prayerfully pull together your creative outlet along with the different areas we have covered.

Enter a time of prayerful organization. Use these succinct questions to help bring you back to previous activities. Set a one-minute timer for each question, ask God to guide you, quiet your mind for a few seconds, then write one sentence before moving on to the next question.

1. **Your Life's Purpose:** Why do you believe you're here? What is your overarching goal?
2. **Your Passions:** What activities or causes do you feel deeply about?
3. **Your Strengths:** What are your unique talents and abilities?
4. **Your Influences:** Who are the greatest influence in your life?
5. **Your Areas for Growth:** In what areas do you want to improve?
6. **Your Core Values:** What principles guide your decisions and actions?
7. **Your Stewardship:** What role does money plan in your life?
8. **Your Legacy:** What do you want to be

remembered for?

9. **Your Contribution to Others:** How do you want to impact the people around you?

10. **Your Vision:** What does success look like in your personal and professional life?

11. **Your Goals:** What specific, measurable objectives do you aim to achieve?

12. **Your Commitment to Action:** How do you envision your mission statement influencing your life?

Use this extra space to add any edits or answers to the specific questions above:

_____

_____

_____

_____

_____

_____

_____

_____

_____

_____

_____
_____
_____
_____
_____
_____
_____
_____
_____
_____
_____
_____
_____
_____
_____
_____
_____

You are about to bring this all together and
write some drafts of your Personal Mission
Statement. Before doing so, write out a prayer
asking God to guide you.

_____

_____

_____

_____

_____

_____

_____

_____

_____

_____

_____

_____

_____

On the following pages, draft out several variations of your future Personal Mission Statement. This doesn't have to be neat, clean, or final.

_____

_____

_____

_____

_____

_____

_____

_____

_____

_____

_____

_____

_____

_____

_____

_____

_____

_____

_____

_____

_____

_____

_____

_____

_____

_____

_____

_____

_____

Above all else, guard your heart, for everything you do flows from it.

PROVERBS 4:23 (NIV)

How you perceive yourself drives how you show yourself.

MICHAEL ACKER

My God-Given Mission

The time has finally come to write out a final version of your Personal Mission Statement. Commit to writing out your mission statement. More importantly, commit to living out the message.

May God guide you!

_____

_____

_____

_____

_____

_____

_____

_____

_____

_____

In their hearts humans plan their course,
but the Lord establishes their steps.

PROVERBS 16:9 (NIV)

God never said that the journey would be
easy, but He did say that the arrival would
be worthwhile.

MAX LUCADO

Reflect and Adapt

Keep in mind that your Personal Mission Statement is a dynamic document, not set in stone. It's designed to evolve as you do. I find myself revisiting and revising mine every few years to ensure it matches my current path and the latest insights I've gained into who I am and who I aspire to be.

Consistently Reflect and Adapt:

- Store your mission statement where you'll see it often, like in your journal, planner, or a digital note on your smartphone.
- Make it a habit to reflect on your statement at the beginning of each week.
- Plan actions weekly that advance you toward your objectives, ensuring they're in harmony with your stated values.
- Use life's changes as a checkpoint to assess how they fit with your mission statement.
- Embrace the fact that as your insights and circumstances change, so too may your mission statement.
- When revisiting your Personal Mission Statement, ponder these questions:
- Is it still representative of your ideal self?
- Does it push you to grow?
- Are you still inspired by it?

Decide on a schedule for reviewing your mission statement. What method or routine will you employ to facilitate this process?

_____

_____

_____

And consider setting a reminder or ritual for when it's time to refresh your Personal Mission Statement. How will you ensure you remember to reassess and update it as needed?

_____

_____

_____

And we all, who with unveiled faces contemplate the Lord's glory, are being transformed into his image with ever-increasing glory, which comes from the Lord, who is the Spirit.

2 CORINTHIANS 3:18 (NIV)

He is no fool who gives what he cannot keep, to gain what he cannot lose.

JIM ELLIOT

About Author Michael Acker

When Michael was young, his parents became committed followers of Christ, leaving behind drug smuggling and new-age witchcraft. They dedicated their lives to serving God through community involvement such as church, soup kitchens and youth sports and eventually full-time missionary work in Mexico.

Michael's parents' dedication marked his life and helped set him on a path toward ministry. After college and nearly twenty years of pastoral ministry, Michael ventured into corporate training and executive communication coaching, while serving as a volunteer at his local church and in his community.

In 2023, Michael and his wife, Taylor, began a conversation with the leadership board of GO ultimately becoming the Executive Director at GO on the Mission, committed to aiding impoverished children and breaking the cycle of poverty.

A Final Note About GO on the Mission

As you've seen, being "on mission" is a big deal to me. Not only has my personal mission statement been a guiding force in my life, but a mission-driven approach has been integral in my pastoral work and corporate training. So, I see some divine humor in being invited to serve as the executive director of a top-notch Christian relief organization, aptly named GO on the Mission.

I'm proud of the work we do, encapsulated in our mission statement:

> "GO on the Mission equips impoverished children to conquer the cycle of poverty through holistic Christ-centered care, enabling them to become followers of Christ who bring hope and healing to their worlds."

There are many great organizations out there, but I was drawn to GO because of our commitment to listen to the needs articulated by our in-country partners. We approach each community with open ears instead of preconceived solutions, ready to collaborate on strategies that address the root causes of poverty. Our unique partnership model empowers our brothers and sisters overseas, increases self-reliance, and creates long-lasting solutions that build a better future for people we serve.

I'd love to see if your God-given mission includes participating—above and beyond your commitment to your local church—in our mission perhaps through our Dollar-Thirty Day challenge or one of our trips or through child sponsorship. Curious? Visit us at www. goonthemission.com.

Finally, I'd love to hear how this guide has been helpful to you on your journey to define and articulate your personal mission statement: michael.acker@goonthemission.com

Find more resources, including absolutely free PDFs, videos, devotionals, sermon series, and more at our mission vault.

https://vault.goonthemission.com

May God bless and guide you in your mission and its unique part in His great mission!

Life on Purpose